# Washington's Birthday

Kelly Rodgers

## Consultants

**Diana Cordray**
**Education Center Manager**
George Washington's
  Mount Vernon

**Shelley Scudder**
**Gifted Education Teacher**
Broward County Schools

**Caryn Williams, M.S.Ed.**
Madison County Schools
Huntsville, AL

**Publishing Credits**

Conni Medina, M.A.Ed., *Managing Editor*
Lee Aucoin, *Creative Director*
Torrey Maloof, *Editor*
Marissa Rodriguez, *Designer*
Stephanie Reid, *Photo Editor*
Rachelle Cracchiolo, M.S.Ed., *Publisher*

**Image Credits:** pp. 11, 19 Alamy;
p. 7 Album/Prisma/Newscom;
pp. 10, 20 The Bridgeman Art Library;
p. 9 Getty Images; p. 22 Gilbert Charles
Stuart, 1976; p. 5 JoeInSouthernCA
(CC-BY-ND)/Flickr; p. 29 (bottom) Joey Rice;
p. 6 The Library of Congress
[LC-USZC2-3793]; p. 8 The Library of
Congress [LC-DIG-pga-02152]; p. 14–15 The
Library of Congress [ LC-USZC4-2737]; p. 16 The
Library of Congress [LC-USZC4-2135]; p. 17
The Library of Congress [LC-USZC2-3310];
p. 21(top) The Library of Congress
[LC-USZC4-10314]; p. 23 The Library of
Congress [ LC-USZC4-12934]; pp. 12, 18–19,
32 Picture History/Newscom; p. 13 Public
Domain; p. 24 The Orange County Register/
Newscom; p. 25 UPI/Newscom; All other
images from Shutterstock.

## Teacher Created Materials
5301 Oceanus Drive
Huntington Beach, CA  92649-1030
http://www.tcmpub.com
**ISBN 978-1-4333-6990-2**
© 2014 Teacher Created Materials, Inc.

# Table of Contents

# George Is All Around

His face is on the one-dollar bill. It is on the quarter, too. His picture may be on your classroom wall. George Washington is all around!

This school honors George with its name.

Cities are named after him. Streets are named after him, too. Even some schools share his name. His birthday is a holiday. Do you know why we **celebrate** (SEL-uh-breyt) George's birthday every year?

George was a great leader during the American Revolution (rev-uh-LOO-shuhn). This was the war that made the United States its own country. George was also the first president of the United States.

George leads the army in the American Revolution.

George was a brave man. He was honest, and he worked hard. Today, he is known as the father of our country.

George Washington

## George's Wig

Many people think George wore a wig. But he did not. He added powder to his light brown hair to make it look white. Many people wore their hair like this in George's time.

# Young George

George was born on February 22, 1732. He grew up in the Virginia **colony** (KOL-uh-nee). A colony is an area ruled by another country. King George of Great Britain ruled the 13 colonies in America.

This is young George with his father.

George grew tall and strong. He learned to be a land **surveyor** (ser-VEY-er). This is someone who studies land. Later, George became a farmer.

**Militia Man**

George was also an officer in the Virginia militia (mi-LISH-uh). A militia is like an army that is used in emergencies (ih-MUR-juhn-seez).

George surveys the land.

In 1759, George married Martha. Together, they made a home at Mount Vernon. Mount Vernon was the Washington family farm.

This is George and Martha getting married.

George loved working on his farm. He always tried to find new ways to grow crops. His main crop was wheat.

George works on his farm.

George was also a leader in Virginia. People liked George. He was calm and smart. He helped make new laws for Virginia.

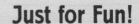

This is George when he was a young man.

George did not like the laws that King George made for the colonies. He thought the king was being unfair. George wanted the colonies to be free.

King George

# War!

In 1775, fights broke out between the **colonists** (KOL-uh-nists) and soldiers (SOHL-jerz) from Great Britain. This started the American Revolution. The colonies were now at war with Great Britain.

George leads the American Army.

George went to Philadelphia (fil-uh-DEL-fee-uh). There, he met with leaders from the other colonies. They chose George to lead their army.

## First Fights

The fights that started the American Revolution took place on April 19, 1775. They were in the cities of Lexington and Concord in Massachusetts (mas-uh-CHOO-sits).

These are American soldiers.

George's soldiers were not well trained. The British Army was big and strong. They had fought in many wars. George's army worked hard. They fought for eight long years. They won some battles. But they lost some, too.

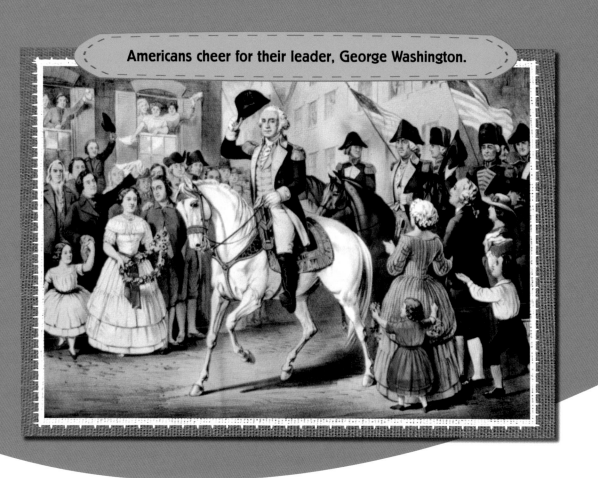
Americans cheer for their leader, George Washington.

George proved to be a strong leader. In 1783, the war ended. George's army had won! The colonies were free. They were a new country called the United States of America.

George knew the new country needed a fair **government** (GUHV-ern-muhnt). It also needed new laws. In 1787, leaders met to make plans for the future. They asked George to lead the meeting.

George helps the leaders write the Constitution.

Next, the leaders wrote the United States **Constitution** (kon-sti-TOO-shuhn). This is the main set of laws for the country. It said there would be a president, not a king.

This is the Constitution.

George becomes the first president of the United States.

# President Washington

The country now needed a president. All the leaders **voted** for George. He became the first president of the United States.

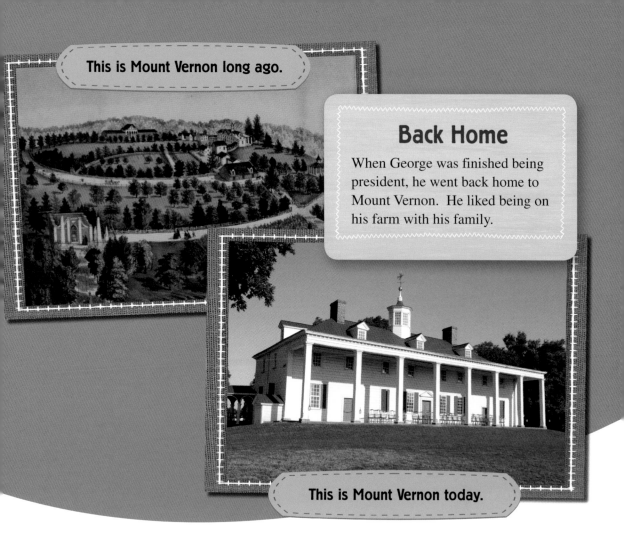

This is Mount Vernon long ago.

## Back Home

When George was finished being president, he went back home to Mount Vernon. He liked being on his farm with his family.

This is Mount Vernon today.

George knew he had a big job. He worked hard. He listened to what the people wanted. For eight years, he helped the new country grow strong.

# American Holiday

Americans **respected** George. He had done so much for them. He helped lead the colonies to freedom. He helped form the new country. Then, he served as the first president. George was a hero.

This is George as president.

Americans wanted to **honor** George. In 1879, his birthday became a holiday. This way, future Americans would learn about George. They would see him as a hero, too.

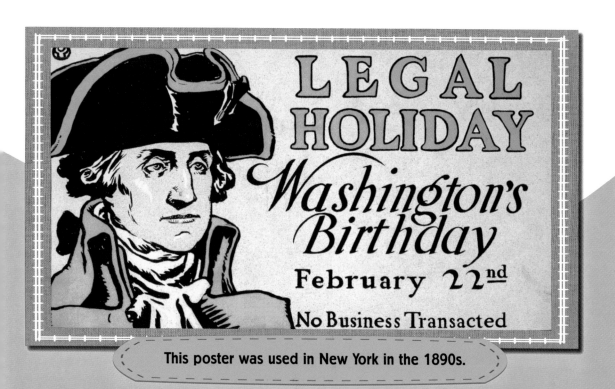

This poster was used in New York in the 1890s.

In 1971, leaders moved some holidays to Mondays. This gave people an extra day off from work and school. George's holiday was moved, too. It is now the third Monday in February.

This man dresses as George to celebrate Presidents' Day.

This day came to be known as Presidents' Day. People across the country celebrate this holiday. They honor all the presidents.

Five presidents take a picture together in 2009.

George was a war hero and a strong leader. He set a good example for future presidents. He also showed people how to be good **citizens** (SIT-uh-zuhns).

This statue shows George as an American hero.

Over 200 years after his death, George Washington still makes Americans proud. He will always be remembered as one of America's greatest leaders.

### Did You Know?

The nation's capital city is named Washington, DC, after George. The capital is where the main offices for the country's government are located.

Washington, DC

# Draw It!

Below is a picture of the Washington Monument in Washington, DC. It was built to honor George Washington. Think of something that you would build to honor George Washington. Draw a picture of it.

This is the Washington Monument.

This girl is drawing a statue of George Washington.

This is her drawing.

# Glossary

**celebrate**—to do something special or fun for an important event or holiday

**citizens**—members of a country or place

**colonists**—people living in an area that is ruled by another country

**colony**—an area ruled by a country far away

**constitution**—a system of beliefs and laws by which a country is governed

**government**—a group of leaders who make choices for a country

**honor**—respect that is given to someone who is admired

**respected**—admired by many people

**surveyor**—a person who inspects and measures the land

**voted**—to have chosen in an election

# Index

# Your Turn!

## Lawmaker

George Washington helped write the Constitution. This is the main set of laws for our country.

Imagine that it is your job to write a constitution for your home. What laws or rules would you write?